101 Homemade Organic Bodycare Recipes

Make Your Own Body Butters, Scrubs, Shampoos, Lotions, Masks, and Bath Recipes

Gabrielle Landreau

Copyright © 2015 Paradise Books

All rights reserved.

In no way is it legal to reproduce, duplicate, or transmit any part of this document in either electronic means or in printed format. Recording of this publication is strictly prohibited and any storage of this document is not allowed unless with written permission from the publisher. All rights reserved.

The information provided herein is stated to be truthful and consistent, in that any liability, in terms of inattention or otherwise, by any usage or abuse of any policies, processes, or directions contained within is the solitary and utter responsibility of the recipient reader. Under no circumstances will any legal responsibility or blame be held against the publisher for any reparation, damages, or monetary loss due to the information herein, either directly or indirectly.
Respective authors own all copyrights not held by the publisher.

The information herein is offered for informational purposes solely, and is universal as so. The presentation of the information is without contract or any type of guarantee assurance.

The trademarks that are used are without any consent, and the publication of the trademark is without permission or backing by the trademark owner. All trademarks and brands within this book are for clarifying purposes only and are owned by the owners themselves, not affiliated with this document.

DISCLAIMER
The information presented on this site is provided for informational purposes only, it is not meant to substitute for medical advice or diagnosis provided by your physician or other medical professional. Do not use this information to diagnose, treat or cure any illness or health condition. If you have, or suspect that you have a medical problem, contact your physician or health care provider.
The author and/or any of their proprietors assume no liability for any injury, illness or adverse affects caused by the misuse and/or use of the information or products presented in this book.

ORGANIC BODYCARE RECIPES

CONTENTS

Introduction To Bodycare Basics — i
Why Organic Body Care? — 1
Organic Face Moisturizers — 7

    Sweet Almond Moisturizer — 8

    Aloe Vera Moisturizer — 9

    Acne Preventing Moisturizer — 10

    Oily Skin Moisturizer — 12

    Citrus Dream Moisturizer — 13

    SPF Daily Moisturizer — 14

    Luscious Lavender Moisturizer — 15

    Minty Green Tea Moisturizer — 16

    Avocado Face Mask Moisturizer — 17

Organic Facial Skin Toners — 19

    Lavender Toner — 20

    Mint Toner — 21

    Dry Skin Toner — 22

    Mask Toner — 23

    Astringent Toner — 24

    Calming Toner — 25

    Sunburn Treating Toner — 26

Acne Fighting Toner	27
Oily Skin Toner	28
Watermelon Toner	29
Scar Minimizing Toner	30
Organic Lip Care	**31**
Basic Lip Balm	32
Peppermint Lip Balm	33
Sweet Lip Balm	34
Mint Chocolate Lip Balm	35
Lemon Exfoliating Lip Balm	36
Pumpkin Exfoliating Lip Balm	37
Tinted Lip Balm	38
Ultra Moisturizing Lip Balm	39
Tinted Lip Stain	40
Plumping Lip Balm	41
Organic Oral Hygiene	**43**
Organic Toothpaste	44
Organic Antiseptic Mouthwash	45
Basic Mouth Rinse	46
Canker Sore and Gum Healing Mouthwash	47
Whitening Paste	48

Organic Bath Recipes — 49

- Sweet Vanilla Bubble Bath — 50
- Calming Bath Soak — 51
- Lavender Bath Melts — 52
- Exfoliating Bath Soak — 53
- Invigorating Citrus Soak — 54
- Tropical Bath Soak — 55
- Good Night Bath Soak — 56
- Raspberry Bath Bomb — 57
- Vanilla Apricot Bath Bomb — 58
- Muscle Relaxing Bath Bomb — 59
- Serenity Bath Bomb — 60
- Congestion Relief Bath Bomb — 61
- Coffee Bath Bomb — 62
- Pear Bath Bomb — 63
- Oatmeal Detox Bath Bomb — 64
- Orange Delight Bath Bomb — 65

Organic Body Butters — 67

- Mango Body Butter — 68
- Vanilla Cocoa Body Butter — 69
- Stretch Mark Erasing Body Butter — 70

Bronzing Body Butter	71
Chocolate Almond Body Butter	72
Skin Tone Evening Body Butter	73
Varicose Vein Improving Body Butter	74
Green Tea Body Butter	75
Dry Skin Healing Body Butter	76
Mint Chocolate Body Butter	77
Tallow Body Butter	78
Eczema Body Butter	79
Ultra Moisturizing Body Butter	80
Mocha Luxury Body Butter	81
Key Lime Body Butter	82
Organic Body Scrubs	83
Mandarin Orange Body Scrub	84
Sugar and Honey Body Scrub	85
Coffee Body Scrub	86
Lime Coconut Body Scrub	87
Vanilla Almond Body Scrub	88
Banana Sugar Body Scrub	89
Grapefruit Body Scrub	90
Lavender Body Scrub	91

Pumpkin Body Scrub for Sensitive Skin	92
Good Morning Body Scrub	93
Rosemary Mint Body Scrub	94
Oatmeal Body Scrub	95
Strawberry Food Scrub	96
Sea Salt Foot Scrub	97
Organic Homemade Shampoo Recipes	99
Basic Shampoo	100
Oily Hair Shampoo	101
Thickening Shampoo	102
Dry Hair Shampoo	103
Lemon Fresh Shampoo	104
Hair Softening Shampoo	105
Dandruff Preventing Shampoo	106
Rosemary Mint Shampoo	107
Organic Homemade Conditioner Recipes	109
Basic Conditioner	110
Spray-in Conditioner	111
Moisturizing Conditioning Mask	112
Hair Growth Conditioning Mask	113

    Deep Conditioning Mask   114

Organic Deodorants   115

    Basic Deodorant   116

    Quick Deodorant   117

    Detoxifying Deodorant   118

    Moisturizing Lavender Deodorant   119

    Spray Deodorant   120

    Antibacterial Spray Deodorant   121

    Powder Deodorant   122

Introduction To Bodycare Basics

When we slather commercial beauty products that contain chemicals all over our bodies, these toxins gets directly absorbed into our skin. This means that most of the beauty care products that you see marketed on television promising to deliver beauty and youth are actually hazardous to our health.

It's simply mind boggling how some of the most dangerous chemicals such as parabens (toxic preservatives), petroleum byproducts (carcinogenic) and phthalates (infertility links) are actually found in the beauty care products that we use every day. Ironically, it's the toxins found in your beauty products that will actually age your skin.

Besides, don't our bodies have enough to deal with fighting off the toxins found in our food and air supply? Why should we burden our bodies further?

That's why as a licensed esthetician and someone who is absolutely obsessed with organics, I created this collection of 101 natural, chemical-free recipes that provide safe and healthy alternatives for personal body care.

Not only will they leave your skin and hair feeling silky smooth, radiant, and healthy but the 101 Organic Body Care Recipes contained in this book-from the shampoos to lotions, the body butters to body scrubs, the facial masks to bath bombs -are simple and very easy to make.

You can easily buy the ingredients at most local stores and you might even already have some in your kitchen cabinets.

Not only are these recipes fun and easy to make but they will only cost you a fraction of the price you'll pay for the store-bought organic ones.

Plus you will absolutely love the way your skin, hair, face, hands and feet will radiate and tingle with health and youthfulness.

Just one try of our Mint Chocolate Lip Balm, Key Lime Body Butter or Vanilla Almond Body Scrub recipes, and I guarantee you'll be hooked for life!

Enjoy!

Gabrielle Landreau

Why Organic Body Care?

Shampoo, deodorants and moisturizers fill the medicine cabinets in just about every home in America. You probably spend a decent percentage of your weekly grocery budget on these and similar items and don't think twice about it because they are a necessity. But let me ask you something. Would you eat these products? Of course not! They are full of chemicals and unsafe materials. But by putting them on your body, you are essentially doing just that. You are consuming them. The chemicals in these products gain full access to your body when you apply them. They are able to penetrate your skin and enter the bloodstream when used as recommended by the companies that produce them.

These products can wreak havoc on your skin and overall health. Allergic reactions are common and skin irritation is not unheard of. Sometimes these chemicals can be carcinogens and cause some serious problems to organs, such as the liver and kidneys. Even the heart can be affected by these toxic synthetics put in your body care products.

Some of the more common chemicals found in bath and body products include several different forms of parabens. These are notorious for causing allergic skin reactions. They are highly toxic but favored by companies due to their low price and ability to extend the shelf life of a product. Almost every product will have fragrance listed as an ingredient, which is a blanket term for hundreds of different combinations of synthetic ingredients that can cause headaches, dizziness and rashes.

Mineral oil is a common ingredient that sounds safe, but when applied causes a barrier over the skin that slows down the development of new and healthy cells. It can also cause acne because it traps any bacteria that was on your skin before you applied it. Propylene glycol, found in shampoo and bubble bath, has been linked to kidney damage and abnormalities of the liver. Next time you pick up your conditioner or favorite body cream, take a moment to read the ingredients. Chances are, you will find one of the dangerous chemicals just mentioned.

So what can you do to avoid the negative side effects of these chemicals? We are not suggesting that you stop bathing or give up your favorite beauty routines. In this book, you will find over one hundred recipes that will enable you to make all of your favorite bath and beauty products right in your own home. You will know every ingredient that goes into each product and will no longer have to worry about what you are putting in your body. These ingredients are easily accessible and won't break the bank. The most common ingredients used in homemade bath products are essential oils, carrier oils, herbs and other natural supplements.

Essential oils are concentrated liquids derived from plants, including leaves, flowers, roots and trees. They are made by extracting the liquid from the solid leaf or flower of the plant, usually by steam or pure expression. Essential oils are popular for their use in aromatherapy, or the use of certain fragrances to improve emotions and state of mind. While this will not be your main motivation for mixing up these products, it is a great extra perk. There are countless varieties of oils and all have different healing properties.

One of their best qualities is that they create an environment where bacteria and viruses find it difficult to live. They are great for the immune system and encourage healthy cell development. Because of the direct concentration of these oils, they will usually need to be diluted in order to be used safely. For this reason, it is not recommended that they be used by pregnant women or people with certain conditions, like epilepsy.

If you are unsure if you should be using these oils, consult with your doctor. If you are using essential oils, always do a spot test on your arm to make sure that there will not be a reaction. Simply take one drop of oil mixed with fifteen drops of carrier oil. Place a small amount on the skin. If there is no redness or irritation after twelve hours, the oil is safe for you to use. Investigate the company that you plan on purchasing your essential oils from.

Unfortunately, this market is not nationally regulated and it is up to you to make sure that you are purchasing high quality ingredients. It is preferred that the oils be made from organic plants. This will ensure that your oil will be pesticide and chemical free.

A carrier oil is needed to dilute the essential oils enough to be safely used, since some oils can be very dangerous if used at their full potency. Examples of carrier oils that you can use are avocado oil, sweet almond oil or the very easily accessible olive oil. Each type of oil has different properties that make them a better match for certain skin and body conditions. Avocado oil is great for sensitive skin. Coconut oil will work wonders on hair that is dry or damaged. Oils with added vitamin E are often recommended because it acts as a natural preservative. Carrier oils have a tendency to become rancid with time and this will help prevent your product from expiring.

Another item that you will need to have to create the recipes in this book is herbs. Some of the most common used herbs are spearmint, rosemary, basil and lavender. They possess fabulous healing properties. These can easily be purchased at your local grocery store or if you enjoy gardening, they can be grown right in your own backyard. It doesn't get much more organic than that! But just as oils are sometimes irritating to the skin, herbs can be as well. To do a spot test, simply rub the fresh herb on a small part of your arm. If the herb is dried, you will need to soak it in a little water first. If you don't notice any redness or irritation after twenty four hours, the herb is safe for you to use.

You may also need some other common kitchen ingredients such as honey, avocado or baking soda. Most ingredients you can find at your local grocery store. Some may need to be purchased at a natural health specialty store and some may be only available online. You will also need some basic kitchen utensils. Measuring cups and spoons, mixing bowls and storage containers should be readily available. You will need an electric mixer, either a stand-up or hand held will work. You will also need a double boiler for several recipes. If you do not have one, simply make your own by placing a saucepan over a bowl of water to melt the necessary ingredients.

Most essential oils do not store well in plastic containers, so invest in dark tinted glass bottles. Most products that you will be making should also be stored in a dark and cool place to prevent bacteria from growing. Make sure that the containers and your hands are completely dry before storing your products.

Always sterilize any containers being used. If a product ends up having an odd smell after storage, it is recommended to dispose of the product as it may be bacteria infested. If the product is made with an ingredient that can spoil, it will need to be stored in the refrigerator and used by the time the ingredient would typically spoil.

By making your own bath and body products at home, you will experience radiant skin, free of irritation and redness. Since these products are antiseptic, you will have clearer skin with less breakouts. You will have the power of knowing what you are exposing your body to and you may even be able to save quite a bit of money. So if you are ready to explore the world of homemade organic bodycare recipes, let's begin.

Organic Face Moisturizers

Moisturizers are important for any type of skin. When applied, they increase the moisture in the top layers of the skin. This protects all of the skin layers and keeps skin looking younger and more radiant.

Sweet Almond Moisturizer

Ingredients:

- ½ cup Shea butter
- 2 tbsp. sweet almond oil
- 15 drops lavender essential oil
- 10 drops rosemary essential oil
- 6 drops carrot seed oil
- 4 drops tea tree essential oil

Directions:

Using a double boiler or similar method, melt Shea butter over medium-low heat. Add sweet almond oil and turn off the heat. Pour into a glass bowl and place it in the freezer until it returns to a solid state without completely freezing (about 15-20 minutes). Once solid, place back at room temperature and add the essential oils. Using a mixer, whip until a light and fluffy consistency appears. Store safely and use on the face as needed.

Aloe Vera Moisturizer

Ingredients:

    1 cup aloe vera gel
    1 cup grated beeswax
    ¼ cup sweet almond oil
    ¼ cup coconut oil
    10 drops grapefruit essential oil

Directions:

Using a double boiler or similar method, melt beeswax and coconut oil. Add in the almond oil. Pour into a blender and let cool until reaching a safe temperature. Mix the grapefruit essential oil into the aloe vera gel. Start the blender and slowly pour in the gel mixture as it whips. Store safely and use on the face as needed.

Acne Preventing Moisturizer

Ingredients:

    3 1/2 tbsp. Shea butter
    2 tbsp. jojoba oil
    3 tbsp. aloe leaf juice
    4 drops lavender essential oil

Directions:

Using a double boiler or similar method, melt the Shea butter and jojoba oil. Once melted, add the aloe leaf juice. Using a mixer, whip the product for 5 minutes and then add the lavender essential oil. Store safely and use every night for clearer skin.

Dry Skin Solving Moisturizer

Ingredients:

    1/3 cup jojoba oil
    2 tbsp. emulsifying wax
    1 tbsp. vegetable glycerin
    1 tsp. vitamin E oil
    1/3 cup rose water
    10 drops grapefruit seed extract
    1 drop ylang ylang essential oil
    3 drops patchouli essential oil
    1 drop rose geranium essential oil
    1 drop frankincense essential oil

Directions:

Using a double boiler or similar method, melt emulsifying wax, jojoba oil and vegetable glycerin. Add the vitamin E oil after removing from heat. Warm the rose water slightly in the microwave and slowly pour into the mix, stirring constantly. Stir in grapefruit seed extract and all essential oils. Store safely, stirring occasionally while cooling to avoid separation, and use to combat dry skin as needed.

Oily Skin Moisturizer

Ingredients:

    1 tbsp. emulsifying wax
    4 tsp. grape seed oil
    ½ tsp. stearic acid
    ½ tsp. vitamin E oil
    1 tbsp. aloe vera gel
    1/3 cup witch hazel
    5 drops grapefruit seed extract
    3 drops lemon essential oil
    5 drops lavender essential oil
    1 drop cedarwood essential oil
    1 drop rose geranium essential oil

Directions:

Using a double boiler or similar method, melt emulsifying wax, grape seed oil and stearic acid. Add vitamin E oil once removing from heat. Warm the aloe vera and witch hazel in the microwave and slowly pour both into the mixture. Once smooth, stir in grapefruit seed extract and essential oils. Store safely and use as needed to combat oily skin.

Citrus Dream Moisturizer

Ingredients:

    6 tbsp. sweet almond oil
    ¼ cup cacao butter
    3 tbsp. Shea butter
    2 tbsp. coconut oil
    1 tbsp. grated beeswax
    2/3 cup floral water
    1/3 cup aloe vera gel
    ½ tsp. vitamin E oil
    1 tsp. vanilla extract
    5 drops orange essential oil
    5 drops lemongrass essential oil

Directions:

Using a double boiler or similar method, melt cacao butter, Shea butter, coconut oil and beeswax. Mix floral water and aloe vera gel together in a separate bowl. Once the butter and oil mixture has cooled, place in blender and slowly add water and gel mixture while blending. The product is done when it has reached a thick and fluffy consistency. Add essential oils, vitamin E oil and vanilla extract. Blend just until mixed. Store safely and use as needed on the face.

SPF Daily Moisturizer

Ingredients:

    ¼ cup coconut oil
    10 drops carrot seed essential oil
    6 drops myrrh essential oil
    4 drops lavender essential oil
    4 drops frankincense essential oil

Directions:

Mix all ingredients in a stand mixer until light and fluffy. The carrot seed will act as a natural SPF for daily use on the face.

Luscious Lavender Moisturizer

Ingredients:

>½ cup coconut oil
>1 tsp. vitamin E oil
>6 drops lavender essential oil

Directions:

Mix all ingredients together until homogeneous. Store safely and use on the face as needed.

Minty Green Tea Moisturizer

Ingredients:

> ½ cup olive oil
> ¼ cup coconut oil
> ¼ cup grated beeswax
> 5 drops mint essential oil
> 5 drops green tea essential oil

Directions:

Using a double boiler or similar method, melt the first three ingredients. Remove from heat and add essential oils. Store safely and use for as a refreshing treat for the face as needed.

Avocado Face Mask Moisturizer

Ingredients:

    3 tbsp. fresh cream
    ¼ of a whole avocado
    1 tbsp. honey

Directions:

Puree all ingredients in a blender or food processor. Use immediately and leave on the face for an hour. Rinse off with warm water and experience the instant nourishment and softness provided by the avocado.

GABRIELLE LANDREAU

Organic Facial Skin Toners

Skin toners should always be part of a daily skin routine. They shrink the pores and add an extra layer of protection over the skin, helping to keep the surface free of bacteria. They also moisturize and keep the skin glowing.

Lavender Toner

Ingredients:

- ½ cup apple cider vinegar
- 2 cups distilled water
- 5 drops lavender essential oil

Directions:

Mix all ingredients together in a bottle. Apply topically with a cotton ball on face and neck daily.

Mint Toner

Ingredients:

    1 1/2 liters of hot water
    Handful of mint leaves

Directions:

Let the leaves soak in the water for at least ten minutes. Strain into a bottle for storage. Apply topically with a cotton ball on face and neck daily.

Dry Skin Toner

Ingredients:

    ½ cup rose water
    1 drop chamomile oil
    1 drop geranium oil

Directions:

Mix all ingredients together in a bottle. Apply topically with a cotton ball on face and neck daily.

Mask Toner

Ingredients:

> ¼ tbsp. vegetable oil
> ¼ tbsp. lemon juice
> 1 tbsp. honey

Directions:

Mix all ingredients together in a bowl and apply immediately to face and neck. Leave on for 10 minutes and rinse off with lukewarm water. Use once a week for a stronger toner.

Astringent Toner

Ingredients:

    2 1/2 cups witch hazel
    1/3 cup apple cider vinegar
    7 drops lavender essential oil

Directions:

Mix all ingredients together in a bottle. Apply topically with a cotton ball on face and neck daily.

Calming Toner

Ingredients:

    3 drops lemon essential oil
    3 drops lavender essential oil
    3 drops distilled water

Directions:

Mix all ingredients together in a bottle. Apply topically with a cotton ball on face and neck daily.

Sunburn Treating Toner

Ingredients:

    ½ cup witch hazel
    10 drops orange essential oil

Directions:

Mix both ingredients together in a bottle. Apply topically with a cotton ball on face and neck daily.

Acne Fighting Toner

Ingredients:

    1 cup water
    1 tsp. baking soda

Directions:

Mix both ingredients together in a bottle. Apply topically with a cotton ball on face and neck daily.

Oily Skin Toner

Ingredients:

    4 oz. water
    10 drops lavender essential oil
    6 drops sandalwood essential oil
    4 drops of tea tree essential oil

Directions:

Mix all ingredients together in a bottle. Apply topically with a cotton ball on face and neck daily.

Watermelon Toner

Ingredients:

    2 tbs fresh watermelon juice
    2 tbs distilled water
    1 tbs vodka

Directions:

Mix all ingredients together in a bottle. Apply topically with a cotton ball on face and neck daily. The watermelon is a great source of vitamins for the skin.

Scar Minimizing Toner

Ingredients:

    ¾ cup witch hazel
    ¼ cup lemon juice
    1 cup peppermint tea

Directions:

Mix all ingredients together in a bottle. Apply topically with a cotton ball on face and neck daily.

Organic Lip Care

The lips are a delicate part of the body. Use these recipes to keep them soft and moisturized and avoid dry, cracked lips.

Basic Lip Balm

Ingredients:

    1 tbsp. grated beeswax
    1 tbsp. coconut oil
    Dash of honey
    ½ tsp. vitamin E oil
    2 drops of desired essential oil

Directions:

Using a double boiler or similar method, melt beeswax, adding coconut oil and honey when it is half melted. After completely melted, stir in vitamin E and essential oil. Pour into a safe container and let set. Apply as needed.

Peppermint Lip Balm

Ingredients:

>1 tbsp. grated beeswax
>2 tbsp. sweet almond oil
>8 drops peppermint essential oil

Directions:

Using a double boiler or similar method, melt beeswax and almond oil together. Remove from heat and stir in peppermint oil. Pour into a safe container and let set. Apply as needed.

Sweet Lip Balm

Ingredients:

    4 tbsp. coconut oil
    3 tbsp. Shea butter
    1 tbsp. grated beeswax
    1 squirt of prepared Kool-aid in desired shade

Directions:

Using a double boiler or similar method, melt the first three ingredients until homogeneous. Stir in Kool-aid. Pour into a safe container and let set. Apply as needed.

Mint Chocolate Lip Balm

Ingredients:

    1 tsp. coconut oil
    1 tsp. Sweet almond oil
    1 tsp. cocoa butter
    3 drops vitamin E oil
    3 drops peppermint extract
    4 semisweet chocolate chips

Directions:

Using a double boiler or similar method, melt all ingredients slowly until combined. Pour into a safe container and let set. Apply as needed.

Lemon Exfoliating Lip Balm

Ingredients:

    1 tsp. coconut oil
    1 tsp. honey
    2 tbsp. granulated sugar
    Dash of lemon juice

Directions:

Mix all ingredients together and store in a safe container. Use with a gentle circular motion across the lips to exfoliate. Rinse with water.

Pumpkin Exfoliating Lip Balm

Ingredients:

    2 tbsp. coconut oil
    1 tbsp. honey
    1 tbsp. brown sugar
    1 tsp. pumpkin pie spice

Directions:

Mix all ingredients together and store in a safe container. Use with a gentle circular motion across the lips to exfoliate. Rinse with water.

Tinted Lip Balm

Ingredients:

    2 tbsp. coconut oil
    1 tbsp. grated beeswax
    1 tbsp. Shea butter
    1/8 tsp. beet root powder for a red tint OR
    ¼ tsp. cocoa powder for brown tint

Directions:

Using a double boiler or similar method, melt the first 3 ingredients together. Carefully stir in desired color. Pour into a safe container and let set. Apply as needed.

Ultra Moisturizing Lip Balm

Ingredients:

    3 tbsp. grated beeswax
    2 tbsp. coconut oil
    ¼ cup sunflower oil
    8 drops vitamin E oil
    2 drops rosemary essential oil
    12 drops peppermint essential oil
    small dab of lanolin (do not use in excess)

Directions:

Using a double boiler or similar method, melt the first 3 ingredients together. Carefully stir in vitamin E, oils and lanolin. Pour into a safe container and let set. Apply as needed.

Tinted Lip Stain

Ingredients:

    5 raspberries
    5 blackberries
    1 tsp. olive oil

Directions:

Slightly mash berries in a bowl. Add olive oil and finish mashing. Strain into a safe container and store in the refrigerator between uses.

Plumping Lip Balm

Ingredients:

    2 tbsp. grated beeswax
    1 tbsp. Shea butter
    1 tbsp. mango butter
    ½ tbsp. cocoa butter
    1 tbsp. sweet almond oil
    ½ tbsp. honey
    12 drops peppermint essential oil
    6 drops cinnamon bark essential oil
    8 drops vanilla essential oil

Directions:

Using a double boiler or similar method, melt the first 4 ingredients together. Stir in almond oil, honey and essential oils. Pour into a safe container and let set. Apply as needed.

GABRIELLE LANDREAU

Organic Oral Hygiene

Toothpaste and mouthwash are filled with toxic chemicals. Use these natural substitutes and experience what a truly clean mouth feels like.

Organic Toothpaste

Ingredients:

    5 tbsp. calcium powder
    2 tbsp. baking soda
    4 tbsp. coconut oil
    essential oils for taste as desired

Directions:

Mix the powders together and add oil until desired consistency is reached. Add oils if they are being used to aid in taste. Store in a safe container. Use a cotton swab or spoon to remove from container and put on toothbrush.

Organic Antiseptic Mouthwash

Ingredients:

    1 ½ cup filtered water
    1 tsp. sea salt
    1 tsp. calcium magnesium powder
    2 drops spearmint essential oil
    2 drops cinnamon essential oil
    2 drops peppermint essential oil
    2 drops clove essential oil
    2 drops myrrh essential oil

Directions:

Mix all ingredients in a glass bottle. Shake before each use. A new batch should be made weekly.

Basic Mouth Rinse

Ingredients:

    1 cup water
    2 tbsp. apple cider vinegar

Directions:

Combine and store in a glass jar. Shake before each use. This rinse will not spoil and can be used daily.

Canker Sore and Gum Healing Mouthwash

Ingredients:

    ½ cup aloe vera juice
    ¼ cup distilled water
    1/2 tbsp. witch hazel
    1 tsp. baking soda
    10 drops peppermint essential oil

Directions:

Mix all ingredients in a glass bottle. Shake before each use. Use for two weeks before making a new batch.

Whitening Paste

Ingredients:

    1 strawberry
    ½ tsp. baking soda

Directions:

Cut strawberry up very small and mash in a bowl. Add baking soda and mix well. Using a cotton swab, apply directly to each tooth and let the paste sit for 5 minutes. Clean each tooth with a toothbrush before rinsing. This treatment may be used twice .

Organic Bath Recipes

At the end of a long day, there is nothing more relaxing than a bubble bath. But before you reach for your store bought bubble maker, look over these recipes and see how easy it is to make a fabulous smelling and relaxing bath soak or even a fun bath bomb.

Sweet Vanilla Bubble Bath

Ingredients:
½ cup light almond oil
¼ cup honey
½ cup mild liquid soap
1 egg white
1 tbsp. vanilla extract

Directions:

Combine all ingredients and store in a glass container. Pour ¼ cup of the product under running water. Keep in the refrigerator between uses.

Calming Bath Soak

Ingredients:

    1 cup Epson salt
    ¾ tbsp. kelp powder
    ½ tbsp. powdered grapefruit peel
    ¼ tbsp. spirulina powder
    4 tbsp. olive oil
    60 drops rosemary essential oil
    30 drops juniper essential oil
    20 drops eucalyptus essential oil

Directions:

Combine all ingredients and store in a glass container. Pour ¼ cup of the product under running water. Use within two months.

Lavender Bath Melts

Ingredients:

    1/2 cup Shea butter
    1/4 cup cocoa butter
    2 drops lavender essential oil per melt
    2 tsp. dried lavender flowers
    2 tsp. chamomile tea

Directions:

Using a double boiler or similar method, melt butters together. Add tea and dried flowers, stirring to combine. Pour into silicone molds and add 2 drops of lavender essential oil to each. Place in refrigerator to set overnight. Use one melt per bath.

Exfoliating Bath Soak

Ingredients:

    1 1/2 cups liquid castile soap
    ½ tbsp. white sugar
    2 tbsp. vegetable glycerin
    6 drops vanilla essential oil
    5 drops food coloring (optional)

Directions:

Combine all ingredients and store in a glass container. Pour ¼ cup of the product under running water.

Invigorating Citrus Soak

Ingredients:

    1 1/2 cup liquid castile soap
    ½ tbsp. white sugar
    2 tbsp. vegetable glycerin
    5 drops bergamot essential oil
    4 drops orange essential oil
    1 drop rose geranium oil
    5 drops food coloring (optional)

Directions:

Combine all ingredients and store in a glass container. Pour ¼ cup of the product under running water.

Tropical Bath Soak

Ingredients:

> ½ cup sugar
> ¼ cup chopped raw mango
> 3 tbsp. coconut oil
> 4 drops orange essential oil

Directions:

Chop mango very fine. Mix with sugar, coconut oil and essential oil. Use immediately. Pour under water during bath.

Good Night Bath Soak

Ingredients:

    1 1/2 cups liquid castile soap
    ½ tbsp. white sugar
    2 tbsp. vegetable glycerin
    5 drops lavender essential oil
    4 drops lemon essential oil
    1 drop chamomile essential oil
    5 drops food coloring (optional)

Directions:

Combine all ingredients and store in a glass container. Pour ¼ cup of the product under running water.

Raspberry Bath Bomb

Ingredients:

- 2 cups baking soda
- 1 cup citric acid
- 3 tbsp. kaolin clay
- 4 tbsp. sweet almond oil
- 1 tbsp. raspberry fragrance oil
- 1 tbsp. witch hazel
- 3 drops red food coloring

Directions:

Mix the baking soda, citric acid and kaolin clay together until there are no clumps. Add sweet almond oil, raspberry fragrance, witch hazel and food coloring. Mix between fingers until it holds a shape. Press into silicon molds. Dry for a total of 24 hours, removing the bath bomb from the mold to air dry for the last 8-10 hours.

Vanilla Apricot Bath Bomb

Ingredients:

    2 tbsp. baking soda
    1 tbsp. cornstarch
    ½ tbsp. citric acid
    1 tbsp. Epsom salt
    ¼ tsp. vanilla essential oil
    ¾ tsp. apricot essential oil
    3 drops yellow food coloring

Directions:

Mix the baking soda, cornstarch, citric acid and Epsom salt together until there are no clumps. Add essential oils and food coloring. Mix between fingers until it holds a shape. Press into silicon molds. Dry for a total of 24 hours, removing the bath bomb from the mold to air dry for the last 8-10 hours.

Muscle Relaxing Bath Bomb

Ingredients:

    2 tbsp. baking soda
    1 tbsp. cornstarch
    ½ tbsp. citric acid
    1 tbsp. Epsom salt
    ¼ tsp. pine essential oil
    ¾ tsp. sandalwood essential oil
    3 drops red food coloring

Directions:

Mix the baking soda, cornstarch, citric acid and Epsom salt together until there are no clumps. Add essential oils and food coloring. Mix between fingers until it holds a shape. Press into silicon molds. Dry for a total of 24 hours, removing the bath bomb from the mold to air dry for the last 8-10 hours.

Serenity Bath Bomb

Ingredients:

    2 tbsp. baking soda
    1 tbsp. cornstarch
    ½ tbsp. citric acid
    1 tbsp. Epsom salt
    ¼ tsp. avocado oil
    ¼ tsp. frankincense essential oil
    ½ tsp. coconut essential oil

Directions:

Mix the baking soda, cornstarch, citric acid and Epsom salt together until there are no clumps. Add avocado oil and essential oils. Mix between fingers until it holds a shape. Press into silicon molds. Dry for a total of 24 hours, removing the bath bomb from the mold to air dry for the last 8-10 hours.

Congestion Relief Bath Bomb

Ingredients:

    2 cups baking soda
    1 cup cornstarch
    1 cup citric acid
    2 tbsp. olive oil
    ½ tsp. peppermint essential oil
    ½ tsp. eucalyptus essential oil
    ½ tsp. lavender essential oil
    ½ cup witch hazel
    3 drops blue food coloring

Directions:

Mix the baking soda, cornstarch and citric acid together until there are no clumps. Add olive oils, essential oils, witch hazel and food coloring. Mix between fingers until it holds a shape. Press into silicon molds. Dry for a total of 24 hours, removing the bath bomb from the mold to air dry for the last 8-10 hours.

Coffee Bath Bomb

Ingredients:

    2 cups baking soda
    1 cup citric acid
    1 tbsp. coffee grounds
    3 tbsp. kaolin clay
    4 tbsp. cocoa butter, melted
    1 tbsp. witch hazel
    3 drops red food coloring

Directions:

Mix the baking soda, citric acid, coffee grounds and kaolin clay together until there are no clumps. Add cocoa butter, witch hazel and food coloring. Mix between fingers until it holds a shape. Press into silicon molds. Dry for a total of 24 hours, removing the bath bomb from the mold to air dry for the last 8-10 hours.

Pear Bath Bomb

Ingredients:

    1 cup baking soda
    1 cup cornstarch
    1 cup citric acid
    ¼ cup Epsom salt
    1 tbsp. pear essential oil
    3 drops green food coloring

Directions:

Mix the baking soda, cornstarch, citric acid and Epsom salt together until there are no clumps. Add essential oil and food coloring. Mix between fingers until it holds a shape. Press into silicon molds. Dry for a total of 24 hours, removing the bath bomb from the mold to air dry for the last 8-10 hours.

Oatmeal Detox Bath Bomb

Ingredients:

- ¼ cup baking soda
- 2 tbsp. citric acid
- 2 tbsp. cornstarch
- ¼ cup oatmeal
- 2 tbsp. olive oil
- 1 tsp. lavender essential oil

Directions:

Mix the baking soda, cornstarch, citric acid and oatmeal together until there are no clumps. Add olive oil and essential oil. Mix between fingers until it holds a shape. Press into silicon molds. Dry for a total of 24 hours, removing the bath bomb from the mold to air dry for the last 8-10 hours.

Orange Delight Bath Bomb

Ingredients:

    2 tbsp. baking soda
    1 tbsp. cornstarch
    ½ tbsp. citric acid
    1 tbsp. Epsom salt
    ¾ tsp. olive oil
    ¼ tsp. mandarin orange essential oil
    Few drops orange food color

Directions:

Mix the baking soda, cornstarch, citric acid and Epsom salt together until there are no clumps. Add olive oil, essential oil and food coloring. Mix between fingers until it holds a shape. Press into silicon molds. Dry for a total of 24 hours, removing the bath bomb from the mold to air dry for the last 8-10 hours.

GABRIELLE LANDREAU

Organic Body Butters

Body butters are luxurious spa treatments for your skin. Now you can make a wide selection of natural body butters that your skin will thank you for.

Mango Body Butter

Ingredients:

- ½ cup Shea butter
- ½ cup mango butter
- ½ cup coconut oil
- ½ cup jojoba oil
- 20 drops peppermint oil

Directions:

Using a double boiler or similar method, combine all ingredients except for the essential oils. Once melted, place the mix into the refrigerator until cool. The mixture should appear cloudy (usually about 1 hour). Remove from the refrigerator and add essential oils. Using a mixer, whip mixture until it is light and fluffy. Store in a safe container and use often as desired.

Vanilla Cocoa Body Butter

Ingredients:

    1 cup cocoa butter
    ½ cup sweet almond oil
    ½ cup coconut oil
    1 vanilla bean

Directions:

Using a double boiler or similar method, melt cocoa butter and coconut oil. Remove from heat and cool 30 minutes. Grind the vanilla bean in a food processor. Stir sweet almond oil and the ground vanilla bean into the mix. Place in the refrigerator for approximately 1 hour, until cloudy in appearance. Using a mixer, whip until fluffy. Store in a safe container and use as often as desired.

Stretch Mark Erasing Body Butter

Ingredients:

    2 oz Shea butter
    2 oz evening primrose oil
    10 drops jasmine essential oil
    10 drops frankincense essential oil

Directions:

Using a double boiler or similar method, melt the Shea butter. Once melted, place them into the refrigerator until cool. The mixture should appear cloudy (usually about 1 hour). Remove from the refrigerator and add essential oils. Using a mixer, whip mixture until it is light and fluffy. Store in a safe container and use as often as desired.

Bronzing Body Butter

Ingredients:

    1 cup Shea butter
    ½ cup coconut oil
    ½ cup olive oil
    1-2 tbsp. cocoa powder
    1 tsp. vitamin e oil
    8 drops peppermint oil

Directions:

Using a double boiler or similar method, melt Shea butter and coconut oil. Let cool slightly and mix in olive oil, cocoa powder, and essential oil and vitamin e oil. Place in the refrigerator for about an hour (until mixture appears cloudy). Remove and use a mixer to whip until light and fluffy. Store in a safe container and use as often as desired.

Chocolate Almond Body Butter

Ingredients:

    1 cup cocoa butter
    2 tbsp. almond oil
    8 drops vitamin e
    8 drops wild orange deTerra essential oil

Directions:

Melt the cocoa butter using a double boiler. Cool and slowly add almond oil while whipping with a mixer until fluffy. Add in vitamin E oil and essential oils. Store in a safe container and use as often as desired.

Skin Tone Evening Body Butter

Ingredients:

    ½ cup Shea butter
    ½ cup coconut oil
    ½ cup kokum butter
    1/4 cup avocado oil
    2 tbsp. rose hip essential oil
    2 tbsp. arnica essential oil

Directions:

Using a double boiler of similar method, melt all ingredients. Put in the refrigerator to cool for about an hour, or until the mixture appears cloudy. Remove and using a mixer, whip until light and fluffy. Store in a safe container and use as often as desired.

Varicose Vein Improving Body Butter

Ingredients:

    ¼ cup coconut oil
    ½ cup Shea butter
    ¼ cup jojoba oil
    10 drops cypress essential oil
    10 drops lemon essential oil
    5 drops fennel essential oil
    5 drops helichrysum essential oil
    1 tbsp. vitamin E oil

Directions:

Using a double boiler or similar method, melt Shea butter and coconut oil. Pour in jojoba oil, vitamin E oil and essential oils. Stir well. Put in the refrigerator for about an hour, or until the mixture appears cloudy. Remove and use a mixer to whip until fluffy. Store in a safe container and use to help varicose veins. Always massage the veins with the butter towards the heart.

Green Tea Body Butter

Ingredients:

- 1 ½ cup Shea butter
- 1 bag used green tea
- ¾ cup olive oil
- 14 drops jasmine essential oil
- 1 tsp. vitamin E oil

Directions:

Using a double boiler or similar method, melt Shea butter. Pour in olive oil and the used contents of a green tea bag. Stir well and then allow to cool to room temperature. Place in freezer for 15 minutes and then add the vitamin E oil and jasmine essential oil. Stir well and store in a safe container. Use as often as desired.

Dry Skin Healing Body Butter

Ingredients:

    1 tbsp. sesame oil
    2 1/2 tbsp. cocoa butter
    1 tbsp. coconut oil
    1 tbsp. grated beeswax
    2 tbsp. almond oil

Directions:

Using a double boiler or similar method, melt cocoa butter, coconut oil and beeswax. Stir in almond oil and sesame oil and place in the refrigerator for about an hour, or until the mixture appears cloudy. Using a mixer, whip until fluffy. Store in a safe container and use as often as desired. This is a necessity for skin during a cold and dry winter.

Mint Chocolate Body Butter

Ingredients:

½ cup cocoa butter
½ cup coconut oil
½ cup Shea butter
1 tsp. vitamin E oil
½ cup sweet almond oil
3 drops peppermint essential oil

Directions:

Using a double boiler or similar method, met cocoa butter, coconut oil and Shea butter. Stir in vitamin E, almond oil and essential oil. Chill in refrigerator for about an hour, or until the mixture appears cloudy. Using a mixer, whip until fluffy. Store in a safe container and use as often as desired.

Tallow Body Butter

Ingredients:

> ½ cup tallow
> 1 cup Shea butter
> ½ cup jojoba oil
> 2 tsp. vitamin E oil
> 1 tsp. peppermint essential oil

Directions:

Using a double boiler or similar method, melt Shea butter and tallow. Add jojoba oil and stir well. Put in refrigerator for 5 minutes. Add vitamin E oil and peppermint. Place back in the refrigerator for another 30 minutes. Using a mixer, whip until fluffy. Store in a safe container and use as often as desired. Tallow is natural and easily absorbed by the skin, providing intense moisture.

Eczema Body Butter

Ingredients:

¼ cup Shea butter
¼ cup coconut oil
10 drops lavender essential oil
8 drops cedarwood essential oil
3 drops vitamin E

Directions:

Using a double boiler or similar method, melt Shea butter and coconut oil. Once melted, place the mix into the refrigerator until cool. The mixture should appear cloudy (usually about 1 hour). Remove from the refrigerator and add essential oils and vitamin E oil. Using a mixer, whip mixture until it is light and fluffy. Store in a safe container and use often as desired.

Ultra Moisturizing Body Butter

Ingredients:

    4 ounces Shea butter
    ½ ounce vitamin e oil
    ¼ ounces jojoba oil
    1 ounce vegetable glycerin
    2 tsp. aloe vera gel
    1 tbsp. rice powder

Directions:

Mix all ingredients together and whip for about 10 minutes with a mixer until light and fluffy. Store in a safe container and use as often as desired.

Mocha Luxury Body Butter

Ingredients:

    2 tbsp. white cocoa butter
    2 tbsp. dark cocoa butter
    4 tbsp. mango butter
    3 tbsp. olive oil
    4 drops coffee essential oil

Directions:

Using a double boiler or similar method, melt all the butters. Add olive oil and essential oil and put in the refrigerator for about an hour, or until mixture appears cloudy. With a mixer, whip until light and flurry. Store in a safe container and use as often as desired.

Key Lime Body Butter

Ingredients:

- ½ cup coconut oil
- 1 tbsp. olive oil
- 2 tbsp. aloe vera gel
- 20 drops lime essential oil
- 20 drops lemon essential oil

Directions:

Combine all ingredients and whip with a mixer for about 5 minutes, or until fluffy. Store in a safe container and use as often as desired.

Organic Body Scrubs

A body scrub gently exfoliates and removes dead skin cells from the surface, leaving a smooth and silky feeling. These are made with all natural ingredients that will leave your skin glowing.

Mandarin Orange Body Scrub

Ingredients:

    3 cups white sugar
    1 cup + 2 tbsp. olive oil
    10 drops mandarin essential oil

Directions:

Combine all ingredients and store in a glass jar in a cool and dark place. Use as needed to help remove rough skin.

Sugar and Honey Body Scrub

Ingredients:

    2 cups brown sugar
    ½ cup olive oil
    ¼ cup honey

Directions:

Combine all ingredients and store in a glass jar in a cool and dark place. Use as needed to help remove rough skin.

Coffee Body Scrub

Ingredients:

>   ¼ cup grape seed oil
>   1/3 cup brown sugar
>   3 tbsp. coffee grounds
>   ¼ tsp. cinnamon

Directions:

Combine all ingredients and store in a glass jar in a cool and dark place. Use as needed to help remove rough skin.

Lime Coconut Body Scrub

Ingredients:

    ¼ cup coconut oil
    1 cup white sugar
    1 tbsp. shredded coconut
    1 tbsp. lime zest
    2 drops coconut extract

Directions:

Combine all ingredients and store in a glass jar in a cool and dark place. Use as needed to help remove rough skin.

Vanilla Almond Body Scrub

Ingredients:

> ¼ cup coconut oil
> ½ cup brown sugar
> ½ cup salt
> 1 tbsp. honey
> 1 drop almond extract
> 1 drop vanilla extract

Directions:

Combine all ingredients and store in a glass jar in a cool and dark place. Use as needed to help remove rough skin.

Banana Sugar Body Scrub

Ingredients:

- 1 cup brown sugar
- 3 brown bananas

Directions:

Combine all ingredients and use immediately. The vitamins and minerals from the banana will provide instant glowing skin.

Grapefruit Body Scrub

Ingredients:

    1 cup sugar
    Juice squeezed from half of a grapefruit
    3 tbsp. avocado oil

Directions:

Combine all ingredients and store in the refrigerator for up to a week. Use as needed to help remove rough skin.

Lavender Body Scrub

Ingredients:

    1 cup sea salt
    2-3 sprigs dried lavender
    5 drops lavender essential oil
    1 cup grape seed oil

Directions:

Combine all ingredients and store in a glass jar in a cool and dark place. Use as needed to help remove rough skin.

Pumpkin Body Scrub for Sensitive Skin

Ingredients:

    1 can pumpkin
    1 cup baking soda
    ¼ cup honey

Directions:

Combine all ingredients and store in a glass jar in the refrigerator for up to a week. Use as needed to help remove rough skin.

Good Morning Body Scrub

Ingredients:

    1 cup sugar
    ½ cup melted coconut oil
    8 drops peppermint essential oil
    9 drops orange essential oil
    3 drops tea tree essential oil
    2 drops lemon essential oil
    1 tbsp. honey

Directions:

Combine all ingredients and store in a glass jar in a cool and dark place. Use as needed to help remove rough skin.

Rosemary Mint Body Scrub

Ingredients:

    1 1/2 cup sugar
    ½ cup kosher salt
    1 cup coconut oil
    8 drops rosemary essential oil
    8 drops peppermint essential oil

Directions:

Combine all ingredients and store in a glass jar in a cool and dark place. Use as needed to help remove rough skin.

Good Morning Body Scrub

Ingredients:

   1 cup sugar
   ½ cup melted coconut oil
   8 drops peppermint essential oil
   9 drops orange essential oil
   3 drops tea tree essential oil
   2 drops lemon essential oil
   1 tbsp. honey

Directions:

Combine all ingredients and store in a glass jar in a cool and dark place. Use as needed to help remove rough skin.

Rosemary Mint Body Scrub

Ingredients:

    1 1/2 cup sugar
    ½ cup kosher salt
    1 cup coconut oil
    8 drops rosemary essential oil
    8 drops peppermint essential oil

Directions:

Combine all ingredients and store in a glass jar in a cool and dark place. Use as needed to help remove rough skin.

Oatmeal Body Scrub

Ingredients:

- ¼ cup rolled oats grounded fine
- ¼ cup almonds ground fine
- 1 tbsp. sweet almond oil
- 2 drops chamomile essential oil
- 4 drops rosewood essential oil
- 9 drops palmarosa essential oil

Directions:

Combine all ingredients and store in a glass jar in a cool and dark place. Use as needed to help remove rough skin.

Strawberry Food Scrub

Ingredients:

    2 tsp. sea salt
    2 tbsp. olive oil
    8 fresh strawberries

Directions:

Combine oil and salt with thinly sliced strawberries. Mash into a paste and spread onto feet. Let sit for as long as desired. Rinse clean with warm water.

Sea Salt Foot Scrub

Ingredients:

- 1 cup sea salt
- 4 drops lavender oil
- 4 drops peppermint oil
- 2 drops black pepper oil
- ¼ cup olive oil
- 2 tbsp. apple cider vinegar

Directions:

Mix the first 4 ingredients and store in a dark glass jar. When ready to use, mix 2 tbsp. of the mix with 2 tbsp. apple cider vinegar. Massage into feet for a deep massage and great exfoliating treatment. Rinse and apply olive oil to soften the feet.

GABRIELLE LANDREAU

Organic Homemade Shampoo Recipes

Shampoos are full of sulfates and other ingredients that can actually strip the hair of its natural oils and shine. These all natural alternatives will restore your hair back to its original glory.

Basic Shampoo

Ingredients:

    ¼ cup coconut milk
    1/3 cup liquid castile soap
    20 drops of an essential oil of choice

Directions:

Combine all ingredients in a dark glass bottle. Shake before each use. Rinse well. This will keep for one month.

Oily Hair Shampoo

Ingredients:

> ½ cup liquid castile soap
> ½ tsp. vegetable glycerin
> 5 drops rosemary essential oil
> 4 drops juniper essential oil
> 1 drop cedar wood essential oil

Directions:

Combine all ingredients in a dark glass bottle. Shake before each use. Rinse well.

Thickening Shampoo

Ingredients:

    1 tbsp. baking soda
    1 cup water

Directions:

Mix ingredients together and use as a shampoo for removing build-up, dandruff and excess oil. You can add cornstarch until the mixture reaches your desired thickness to add natural volume to your hair.

Dry Hair Shampoo

Ingredients:

    1 cup castile soap
    2 tbsp. apple cider vinegar
    1 tbsp. tea tree oil
    ¼ cup water

Directions:

Mix all ingredients together in a spray bottle to mist on dry hair for instant moisture.

Lemon Fresh Shampoo

Ingredients:

    1 cup organic shampoo base
    1 tbsp. coconut oil
    20 drops lemon oil

Directions:

Mix shampoo base and coconut oil until fully combined. Add lemon essential oil. Store in a dark glass bottle. Shake before each use. Rinse well.

Hair Softening Shampoo

Ingredients:

- 1 tbsp. honey
- 3 tbsp. filtered water
- 2 drops lavender essential oil
- 2 drops carrot seed oil

Directions:

Combine all ingredients. Use immediately and make fresh each time. The consistency will be runny. Rinse well.

Dandruff Preventing Shampoo

Ingredients:

    ½ cup liquid castile soap
    ½ tsp. vegetable glycerin
    5 drops tea tree essential oil
    2 drops lavender oil
    2 drops rosemary oil

Directions:

Combine all ingredients in a dark glass bottle. Shake before each use. Rinse well.

Rosemary Mint Shampoo

Ingredients:

    ½ cup liquid castile soap
    ½ tsp. vegetable glycerin
    5 drops rosemary essential oil
    3 drops peppermint essential oil
    2 drops bay essential oil

Directions:

Combine all ingredients in a dark glass bottle. Shake before each use. Rinse well.

GABRIELLE LANDREAU

Organic Homemade Conditioner Recipes

These natural conditioners will leave your hair light and full of volume without the build-up of unnatural ingredients.

Basic Conditioner

Ingredients:

    1 cup coconut oil
    1 tsp. vitamin E oil
    1 tsp. jojoba oil
    4 drops lavender essential oil

Directions:

Combine all ingredients and using a mixer, blend on high for 6-8 min. If living in a warmer climate, store in the refrigerator between uses. Use a nickle-sized amount as needed after shampooing.

Spray-in Conditioner

Ingredients:

    1 tbsp. apple cider vinegar
    1 cup water
    7 drops rosemary oil

Directions:

Combine all ingredients in a spray bottle. Shake before each use. This will help to bring back dry and damaged hair to its original shine.

Moisturizing Conditioning Mask

Ingredients:

    2 tbsp. honey
    2 tbsp. glycerin
    2 tbsp. olive oil
    1 large overripe sliced banana

Directions:

Mix all ingredients in a blender. Apply to clean hair. Rinse after 30-50 minutes.

Hair Growth Conditioning Mask

Ingredients:

- 1 egg yolk
- 1 tsp. of olive oil
- Water as needed

Directions:

Whip egg and oil together. Add water slowly to achieve desired consistency. Apply to hair and scalp and leave on for 15-20 minutes. Rinse with cool water. The protein of the egg and minerals in the olive oil will help to stimulate healthy and fast hair growth.

Deep Conditioning Mask

Ingredients:

    3 tbsp. apple cider vinegar
    ¼ cup olive oil
    1 overripe sliced avocado
    ½ cup Shea butter

Directions:

Using a blender, combine all ingredients. Apply to hair and scalp and wrap a towel around to seal. Leave in for 40-50 minutes and rinse clean.

Organic Deodorants

Deodorants have come under the radar lately for their toxic chemicals and the negative effects they can have on your health. Natural deodorants do require a little patience. The body will need to adjust to a chemical free product, but after the detox period, natural deodorants are highly effective.

Basic Deodorant

Ingredients:

    3 tbsp. coconut oil
    3 tbsp. baking soda
    2 tsp. Shea butter
    2 tsp. arrowroot
    Essential oils as desired

Directions:

Using a double boiler or similar method, melt Shea better and coconut oil. After removing from heat, add baking soda and arrowroot. Stir well and then add in any desired essential oils. Pour into a safe container and use daily.

Quick Deodorant

Ingredients:

    6 tbsp. coconut oil
    ¼ cup baking soda
    ¼ cup cornstarch
    essential oils as desired

Directions:

Mix dry ingredients together in a bowl. Add coconut oil and combine. Add essential oils if desired. Store in a safe container and use daily.

Detoxifying Deodorant

Ingredients:

    2 tbsp. coconut oil
    1 tbsp. Shea butter
    ¾ tbsp. almond oil
    ¾ tbsp. grated beeswax
    1 tbsp. arrowroot
    1 tbsp. diatomaceous earth (food grade)
    5 drops vitamin E oil
    20 drops of an essential oil of choice

Directions:

Using a double boiler or similar method, melt the coconut and almond oils, Shea butter and beeswax. Add arrowroot, diatomaceous earth and essential oils after removing from heat. Whisk until fully incorporated. Poor into a safe container and use daily.

Moisturizing Lavender Deodorant

Ingredients:

    3 tbsp. coconut oil
    2 tbsp. Shea butter
    3 tbsp. baking soda
    2 tbsp. cornstarch
    5 drops lavender essential oil

Directions:

Using a double boiler or similar method, melt coconut oil and Shea butter. Add baking soda and cornstarch after removing from heat. Mix in essential oil and transfer to a safe container.

Spray Deodorant

Ingredients:

    witch hazel to fill 2 oz. container
    1 tbsp. magnesium oil
    Pinch of real sea salt
    15 drops lavender essential oil
    5 drops frankincense essential oil

Directions:

Combine salt and essential oils in a spray bottle. Add magnesium oil and fill the rest of the bottle with witch hazel. Shake before each use. This deodorant has a 6 month shelf life.

Antibacterial Spray Deodorant

Ingredients:

    1 tbsp. apple cider vinegar
    filtered water to fill 2 oz. Container
    4 drops rosemary essential oil
    4 drops lavender essential oil

Directions:

Mix all ingredients and add water to a spray bottle. Shake well before each use. Works best if used every evening before bed.

Powder Deodorant

Ingredients:

    1 1/2 cup cornstarch
    ½ cup baking soda
    3 tbsp. dried peppermint leaves, ground very fine
    20 drops peppermint essential oil

Directions:

Mix dry ingredients together until there are no clumps. Slowly add essential oil until smooth. Store in a safe container and use after bathing.

Enjoy!

I hope by now you've had a chance to make a few of the body care recipes contained in this book. If you did then I think you will understand why I am so obsessed with making my own beauty care products. Not only do they feel and smell deliciously amazing but they are so healthy you may just want to eat them.

Don't let the 101 recipes contained in this book overwhelm you. Just start out making your favorite body care products and your favorite scents to get started. Before you know it, you will be a pro at making your own beauty care products from home. You may even decide down the road to market them, who knows?

Whatever you do, don't be afraid to experiment with new combinations of oils and scents. It keeps things funs, exciting and unique. And don't be shy about sharing these recipes as gifts for birthdays and Christmas. Any time you are able to help someone make the move from the toxic, commercial beauty products that are tested on animals to healthy natural products that are aligned with nature- you are giving one of the greatest gifts you can give!

Have Fun!

Gabby

www.ingramcontent.com/pod-product-compliance
Lightning Source LLC
Chambersburg PA
CBHW021446070526
44577CB00002B/287